Jesse Owens
World's Fastest Human

Devon Hind
Kate Bergstresser

Seacoast Publishing
Birmingham, Alabama

Jesse Owens: World's Fastest Human

Published by Seacoast Publishing, Inc.
1149 Mountain Oaks Drive
Birmingham, Alabama 35226

Copyright © 2003 Devon Hind and Kate Bergstresser

All rights reserved.
Reviewers and writers of magazine and newspaper articles are free to quote passages of this book as needed for their work. Otherwise, no part of this book may be reproduced or transmitted in any form or by any means, electronic or mechanical, including photocopying, recording or by any information storage and retrieval system, without the written permission of the publisher.

Library of Congress Card Number: 2002112974

Cover art by Thomas B. Moore

ISBN 1-878561-38-3

To obtain copies of this book, please write or call:
Seacoast Publishing, Inc.
Post Office Box 26492
Birmingham, Alabama 35260
(205) 979-2909

Devon Hind and Kate Bergstresser

Jesse Owens: World's Fastest Human

Dedications

To my Boys Club Director Sam Sheehy: He taught me the value of loyalty and good character.

To my high school teacher Vibeke Eggen: She demanded so much and I learned because of it.

To my parents Myra and Ken Hind: They have always modeled a life of hard work and moral living.

To my track coaches throughout my career—Barry Davis, Bob Oring and John Mitchell: They worked me hard and encouraged me through the good and the bad.

To my wife Mary: She has been my helper and encourager since our high school days.

—Devon Hind

To my God and country: Without which Jesse Owens would not have been able to accomplish all that he did.

To people everywhere: Who take a risk to stand up for the truth and reach their dreams.

—Kate Bergstresser

About The Series

Alabama Roots is a book series designed to provide reading pleasure for young people, to allow readers to better know the men and women who shaped the State of Alabama, and to fill a much-needed void of quality regional non-fiction for students in middle grades.

For years, teachers and librarians have searched for quality biographies about famous people from Alabama. This series is a response to that search. The series will cover a span of time from pre-statehood through the modern day.

The goal of *Alabama Roots* is to provide biographies that are historically accurate and as interesting as the characters whose lives they explore.

The *Alabama Roots* mark assures readers and educators of consistent quality in research, composition, and presentation.

It is a joint publishing project of Seacoast Publishing, Inc., and Will Publishing, Inc., both located in Birmingham, Alabama.

Jesse Owens: World's Fastest Human
Writing This Book

One of the first things that the authors did after being assigned to write about Jesse Owens was travel to The Jesse Owens Museum in Speake, Alabama and spend the entire day looking at the exhibits. From that first visit, they had 19 pages of notes containing dates, accomplishments, quotes and descriptions of uniforms, shoes and pictures that we saw.

They walked through a replica of Jesse's house and tried to imagine what it would have been like to live there. They also bought two books from the museum that were recommended as the best reference sources and read each of them more than once. One was Jesse Owens' autobiography (assisted by author Paul Neimark) called *Jesse—The Man Who Outran Hitler*. The other book was written by Tony Gentry and titled *Jesse Owens—Olympic Superstar*. The authors had a lot of facts from the museum, but these books brought their character to life. When they needed more information than they had in their notes or resource books, they searched the Internet.

After completing their research, they decided what parts of Jesse's life they wanted to include in the book. They planned their chapters and made a list of the topics that they wanted to cover in each chapter. They originally planned to have twelve chapters.

Devon Hind and Kate Bergstresser

Ms. Bergstresser was assigned to write chapter one. When the rough draft of chapter one was completed, Mr. Hind rewrote the chapter using many of Kate's words and ideas. Once it was completed, Mr. Hind continued writing each chapter in consecutive order. Ms. Bergstresser was assigned to write about specific events in Jesse's life. Mr. Hind would take what she had written and blend it in with the chapters he was writing. In this way, all of the book would have the same writing style.

After completing each chapter, the authors asked many friends to read the rough draft. They listened to their suggestions about how to improve the book. They rewrote it many, many times until it met their satisfaction.

Finally, the publisher read the book and made suggestions too. The authors rewrote some parts of the book one last time and checked for typing errors before having it published.

Contents

Treasured Times 9
Please...Stop 15
Christmas Surprise 22
Life In The Big City 29
Rise and Shine 36
Horses Don't Lie 43
Breaking Through the Barrier 50
Wedding Bells 59
A Dream Comes True 62
45 Minutes In History 69
Highs and Lows 76
Olympic Fears 80
Jazze Owens! 88
After the Gold 96
Epilogue 104
About the Authors 118

Treasured Times

IT WAS EARLY, so early on this September morning that the sun was barely creeping over the horizon, dimly lighting the endless fields of cotton.

James Cleveland Owens usually was still asleep.

But not this morning.

He was up. Carefully tiptoeing around nine brothers and sisters sprawled out across the wooden floor.

He wanted to make sure Mama remembered that tonight they would have meat with dinner. In the best years, this poor sharecropper family only had meat thirteen times. Easter. Christmas. Sometimes on the Fourth of July. And on each of the ten children's birthdays.

Today was J.C.'s birthday.

Everybody was going to get meat.

James Cleveland was his name, but everybody called him J.C.

Jesse Owens: World's Fastest Human

Replica of Jesse Owens' birthplace in Oakville, on grounds of Owens' Museum.

He pushed aside the cloth that was a door separating the only two bedrooms in the three-room wooden shack that was the Owens' home. He crept to his mama's side of the bed and watched his parents sleeping peacefully. He stood there staring for what seemed like a long time, hoping that they would just open their eyes. No such luck. J.C. wasn't the kind of boy who could wait a long time for something to happen. He reached over and gently shook his mama. He whispered with pride, "Today is a special day! Do you know why?"

Rolling over and propping up on one elbow his father said with a grin, "Why, I do believe it is my son's birthday, isn't it?"

Mama reached up and put her callused hand

Devon Hind and Kate Bergstresser

gently behind her youngest son's head. She softly massaged the back of his neck as her fingers ran through his hair. He could tell by her touch and the glow in her eyes that he was loved.

"You go on and wake your brothers and sisters," Mama said. "And wash up too. You'll need some breakfast if you want to look like the five-year-old you are."

J.C.'s older brothers and sisters didn't wake with the same enthusiasm that his parents did. They knew that morning light brought another day of hard labor in the fields under the hot Oakville, Alabama sun. The nine-mile walk to and from school was a luxury only enjoyed when children were not needed in the cotton fields. There was work to do on this 12th day of September, 1918 and it had to get done even if it was J.C.'s birthday.

A sharecropper's life was not an easy one. Every day the family got up early and worked the land until daylight was gone.

It was land that they did not even own. Mr. Clannon owned the land. He rented the Owens' their tools, house and the land. The large Owens family plowed the soil. They planted the fields, kept the weeds from taking over and harvested the crops. They were called sharecroppers because they shared a percentage of the crops with Mr. Clannon to pay their rent. By the time Mr. Clannon finished paying the bills and taking his share of the money, there was not much left for the Owens family. That is why meat was on the table only thirteen times each year.

It is also why J.C. only owned two shirts, one for work and one for church.

For the black folks around Oakville, going to church meant the same nine-mile walk as going to school because the church and school were the same building.

But J.C.'s family didn't mind the long walk. It was one of the few times that they could just walk along and talk and tease and play. It was one of the few times they could just have fun and not have to work.

It was during these walks that each brother and sister told about their hopes and dreams for the future. J.C. was always the real dreamer of the family. While the rest of the kids set their eyes on owning a piece of land or marrying a wealthy man, J.C. had his eye on the highest of goals, even as a little boy. James Cleveland Owens wanted to go to college and he made it known to everyone that would listen. His dream brought long peals of laughter from the rest of the family.

Devon Hind and Kate Bergstresser

"You're the one, J.C.," they would say. "Always dreaming the impossible."

While working the fields this birthday, the others asked J.C. what his birthday wish was going to be. It was the same as always. He wanted to go to college. It seemed to make carrying the heavy, drinking water bucket easier if he could think of better times ahead. Times also when he might have the treat of riding to town with his father again and stopping at the store to eat soda crackers and licorice like he'd done once before. This was a happy, memorable fifth birthday for J.C.

The next morning things were different.

Mama noticed a lump in J.C.'s chest, like the one he once had on his leg. He had always been a weak child. He was constantly ill, making it hard at times for the rest of the family to get much work done.

This new lump did not look too good. Everyone worried about it, and would check on it every so often. It was growing. It poked out from his chest more and more. It also grew inward and got so big that soon J.C. had a hard time breathing.

J.C. needed help. But the nearest doctor was 75 miles away. The Owens' could not afford to pay a doctor bill anyway. They never had.

Jesse Owens: World's Fastest Human

But it soon became obvious that if J.C. was going to see his next birthday, something had to be done. J.C.'s eyes became wide with fear when he found out what was about to happen.

Devon Hind and Kate Bergstresser

Please...Stop

THE GROWING LUMP made it so hard for J.C. to breathe that when he lay down at night, the dreadful sounds he made were even louder than the crickets chirping outside in the moonlight. His brothers and sisters tossed and turned as they tried to block the wheezing sounds from their ears.

Before drifting off to sleep one night, J.C. heard his mama and daddy talking in the next room. They were whispering and J.C. strained to hear.

The more he listened, the louder his tiny chest pounded.

"We've got to do something, Henry," his mama said.

"You took one off his leg once, Emma."

"But this one's so big. And near his heart."

J.C. could tell his mama and daddy were worried. He could tell they didn't know what to do, but that they intended to do something.

Jesse Owens: World's Fastest Human

The baby of their family was dying and they knew it. They could wait no longer. J.C.'s mama had always been the doctor around the house and things were no different now. She would have to do what she had put off for so long.

She woke J.C. long before the sun rose the next morning.

She had been holding a knife over the fire for a long time. Two pots of water boiled in the fireplace. All of J.C.'s brothers and sisters were awake too. They knew something was about to happen, and it wasn't going to be good. J.C. knew something was about to happen too, but he was not quite sure what it was.

Then Mama told him.

"I'm going to take off the lump now, J.C." Mama said.

J.C. looked in his mama's eyes with dread, and with a silent plea he begged her not to go through with her plan.

Mama stared back, her eyes filled with tears.

Behind those tears, J.C. saw something else...something that he had always seen. He saw the love that she held deep in her heart for J.C. and every other one of her babies.

J.C. finally understood what was about to happen to him. He also could tell by looking into his mama's eyes that what she was about to do was because she loved him.

"Aw...Mama...no," was all J.C. had the strength to wimper.

Emma Owens had to dig at the lump for a long time, and deep.

"Please...stop," J.C. groaned.

But once she started, there was no way to stop until she had it all.

J.C.'s brothers and sisters held him down while Mama dug and dug. They all were sick to their stomachs from participating in such a dreadful event.

The digging hurt worse than anything J.C. had ever felt before, worse than when he got caught in the animal trap that his daddy had set. It was even worse than the time when the white neighbor boys tried to carve their initials into J.C. before his brothers came to the rescue.

J.C. didn't feel the pain any longer when he finally passed out as Mama finished her task. The lump was finally gone and in its place was a deep hole.

The hole was much deeper than Mama thought it would be, and it began to fill with blood that slowly oozed out. It kept oozing out. The rags Mama used for towels were soon soaked with J.C.'s blood. Everyone

Jesse Owens: World's Fastest Human

looked for scraps of cloth to put over the wound to try and stop the bleeding. They tried burlap sacks and old shirts that were supposed to be on the backs of those working in the fields. They didn't need the shirts just then. No one worked in the field that day. The family watched in fear as the life-giving blood of their tiniest member slowly drained away.

 J.C. floated in and out of consciousness. He was sure that he was dying when he opened his eyes and saw the family surrounding him. There were only two occasions in the Owens' household when the sun was shining outside and work wasn't being done in the fields. One was Christmas day and the other was when someone died. And J.C. was quite sure that it was not Christmas.

 When J.C. didn't die that first day, everyone went out into the fields again. But not Mama. She would not leave J.C.'s side except when she had to go rinse the blood out of the rags. She could hardly keep up with the oozing stream of blood. It just kept coming and coming. J.C. could feel it slowly dribbling down his side, finding its way to the floor. It would pool and then move out across the wooden planks, like a river meandering through the countryside. It kept flowing until someone took another soiled rag and wiped it up.

Devon Hind and Kate Bergstresser

Three days passed and, somehow, James Cleveland Owens was still alive.

He didn't remember a lot of what happened in those three days.

But on a black, moonless night, he remembered waking up.

He could hear something. He wasn't sure what it was.

Even Mama, dead tired from exhaustion, was fast asleep like his brothers and sisters.

But he kept hearing that sound. What was it?

Whatever it was caused him to stir for the first time in three days.

He didn't know why, but he had to find out what that sound was. With blood oozing down his side J.C. raised up to see if he could hear better. But he couldn't.

So with every bit of strength he had left, J.C. dug his tiny nails into those stained wooden floorboards and dragged his limp body toward the door.

He never knew how or why he had the strength to make it, but he finally clawed his way to the front door, leaving a fresh red stain behind him.

On the front porch was J.C.'s father rocking back and forth on his knees, moaning, tears streaming down his face. "You just can't let him die, Lord. You know that it will just kill his mama if he does. And you know that without her the rest of us will die too. Oh Lord, he's the last one who can carry on our name and Mama has always said that he's the special one 'cause he was born when she didn't think it was possible..."

Somehow J.C. found strength from somewhere within himself, when it seemed there was no more strength to find.

He pushed himself up onto his hands and knees. Then he raised himself up to his knees.

He held his arms out and as his daddy paused for breath, J.C. cried out in a faint whisper, "Daddy."

Henry Owens whisked his son up into his arms and pleaded with him, "Pray J.C.! Pray that it would please stop!"

J.C. had walked those nine miles to church many times.

He had watched the rest of his family and friends singing and praying and listening to the preacher all of those Sundays.

He had even followed their example and said the same words that they did and sang the same songs too.

He had tried his hardest to listen to what the man

in the black suit was saying to them, but most of the time he was not quite sure.

But this time, for the first time, James Cleveland remembers truly praying. In his daddy's arms, he prayed. He never did remember what he said or how long he said it. But what he did remember was that when his daddy stood up to take him back inside, the bleeding had stopped.

And it never started up again.

The next morning, J.C. was sitting up and eating.

The day after that he went outside and played.

A few days later, he was back out working in the fields.

Christmas Surprise

JAMES CLEVELAND HEALED, grew stronger and that September of 1919, he celebrated another birthday.

To the surprise of many, he had lived to see his sixth birthday.

It had been a tough year for the Owens family.

A brother and a sister had died.

Another sister left the farm in Oakville for Cleveland, Ohio, to live out her dreams of a big-city life.

It was not a good year for the farm.

The corn and cotton crops didn't earn enough money to cover the rent that Henry owed Mr. Clannon.

Mr. Clannon was angry.

Henry and Emma Owens had done all they could in the fields and it still was not good enough. Mr. Clannon threatened to take their thirty-year-old mule, the only real possession the Owens family had, and sell it if they could not come up with the money they owed.

What was Henry to do? All he knew was sharecropping. He had started young like his father and grandfathers before him, all the way back to slavery days.

The problem of paying Mr. Clannon festered all fall, and still hung heavily over the family as Christmas approached.

Even with tough times, the children were still excited on Christmas Eve. The smell of meat cooking would surely greet them when they woke up. They knew that in years past there had always been a tree to decorate. It did not matter that the tree was a scraggly thing that their daddy had found in the woods. It didn't even matter that the socks they would wear the next day had to be draped over the limbs for decorations. If they were lucky, some colored ribbon or shiny wrapping paper from Mr. Clannon's trash would decorate the tree too. It did not matter that there would not be any presents under their tree. After all, there never had been any.

But that Christmas morning there was no tree to decorate. And there was no sweet aroma of meat cooking either. That Christmas morning held nothing special. It was a day of mouths to feed and little food to put in them. That is why Henry and Emma slipped out of the house that Christmas afternoon. They walked to the only place they could find to talk about important things without the children listening. They walked out into the 40-acres of fields that they worked.

J.C. did not like to be separated from his parents, especially when he didn't know where they were. J.C. had been playing and hadn't noticed when his parents slipped away.

He took off running to find them.

J.C. loved to run. He wasn't very good, but it was the one thing that he could do and no one could stop him. When J.C. ran, the world was his. He could run as fast or as slow as he wanted, in any direction that he desired to go, fighting the wind if he was so inclined.

Running is what made J.C. tick. He loved to feel the power in his legs as the earth moved under his feet. As strange as it may seem, he loved to feel his chest heaving in and out as his lungs burned from the self-inflicted pain. His reward was knowing that he would be better because of the hard work.

So it did not bother J.C. that he had to run to all the corners of the property before finally finding his mama and daddy. He knew that he was not supposed to be there so he hid behind a large rock when he heard their voices.

"Emma, you're talking like J.C. with all those crazy dreams!"

"It's crazy to keep going on like this, Henry!"

"We've got no choice. What other kind of work am I going to do?"

"Other folks have done it," Emma said.

"Yeah. And they've never been heard of again!"

"Why should they come back? There's nothin' here to draw them back. And how could they ever write, Henry? How many colored people knows how to write? Do you think if you stay workin' for the boss here that any of your own younguns will ever learn how to put words on paper? They'll make their mark, an X, just like you have to."

This brought a long silence from J.C.'s daddy.

"But, we'll never be able to make it, Emma. We'll all starve."

"We're all about to starve here, Henry!"

Emma knew that she wanted a better life for her family, but she also respected her husband Henry. She would do whatever he decided. So when Henry Owens announced, "We're stayin' put and that's final," Emma shook her drooping head in defeat. She had done her best to convince Henry and she would try again some day. She would not give up on a better future.

It was at that moment that someone else came running up in a panic. Without thinking, J.C. stood up to see who it was.

"J.C.! What are you doin' here? You better git on home, and quick!" his parents bellowed.

J.C. also respected whatever his daddy had to say. His mama too. So without hesitating, he turned to hurry home. But he didn't hurry too fast so he could hear what the new arrival had to say. It was Jim Turner, a sharecropper from just the other side of their neighbors, the Stepparts.

Jim could hardly get the words out at first because he was so out of breath. "The Stepparts is dead! He and the missus both hung themselves."

That was all J.C. needed to hear. He raced back to the house and spread the word to all of his brothers and sisters.

"You sure? You're gonna be in big trouble if you're lyin' 'bout this one!"

But by the frightened look on J.C.'s face, they knew he was telling the truth. What did it mean? Why would those good hard-working folks do such a thing? None of the children had any answers. They waited to hear what their parents would say.

Three hours is a long time to wait for anything, but at a time like this it seemed like an eternity. Where could they be? What could they be doing?

Henry Owens walked through the door holding his wife's hand behind him. Before the children had time to ask questions, Mama announced, "J.C., go get the mule and run him over to Mr. Clannon's. The rest of you boys gather up all the tools and take them over there too. Me and the girls will be washin' down this house while you're gone."

"How come?" J.C. asked.

"Because I ain't about to leave no one else a dirty house to live in, that's why."

"What do you mean?" J.C. persisted.

"I mean we're headin' for a better life, J.C.," his mama said with a shout. "We're gonna take a train ride!"

"Where we goin', Mama? Montgomery?"

"No. We're goin' much further away than that. We're headin' up there to Cleveland where your sister is. I 'spect there might even be one of those schools up there that you've been a talkin' 'bout too. What do y'all call 'em? College? But if'n ya don't hurry up and git that mule over to Mr. Clannon's, then that mule might just pass on. And then where are we gonna git the money to pay for that train ride? We gotta be outa here by sundown. Now, hurry up!"

J.C. didn't need to hear any more. Neither did his brothers and sisters. They were heading for a better life!

J.C. couldn't get that mule to Mr. Clannon's fast enough. All he could think about was that he would get to go to college some day!

Maybe dreams really do come true after all, he thought.

There was one family member who wasn't filled with excitement that Christmas afternoon. Thirty years of working the fields had netted Henry Owens only the clothes on his back and a skinny, worn out body. He knew sharecropping was a hard life that wouldn't profit him much, but it was a life that he had accepted.

Life outside of Oakville, Alabama had never really existed for him. He stood outside the house wringing his shaking hands, wondering what in the world he had finally agreed to.

Devon Hind and Kate Bergstresser

Life In The Big City

ALMOST EVERYTHING ABOUT CLEVELAND, Ohio was different from Oakville, Alabama.

When J.C. Owens woke up early and peered out the window of his new home he saw paved streets busy with travelers instead of lonely dirt roads. Instead of rows of cotton and corn, there were rows of buildings.

And instead of getting ready to go to the fields, he was washing up to go to school.

J.C. adored school. He was so excited about learning new things. Since the teacher was not sure how much schooling J.C. had in Alabama, she started him in the first grade even though he was older and much taller than the rest of the children in his class at Bolton Elementary School. He advanced quickly, however, to be in the same grade as others his age.

"What is your name?" the teacher asked on J.C.'s

first day at Bolton.

"J.C. Owens," he replied.

"You don't sound like you're from around here," the teacher said. "Where are you from?"

"I'm from way down yonder in Alabama, Ma'am. We took a train that brought me and my family all the way up here. We ain't been here too long yet."

"Well, we're glad to have you in Cleveland, Jesse. I hope you'll be happy here." His teacher then turned to the rest of the class, "I hope the rest of you children will make Jesse feel welcome."

"Hello, Jesse!" a boy shouted.

"Nice to have you here, Jesse," came other greetings.

One of the things that J.C. did not expect to be different was for people to talk so funny. They spoke English, of course, but it sure sounded different in Oakville. What puzzled him most was that everyone thought that he was the one who talked funny and sometimes they teased him about it. He knew that the teacher had mispronounced his name when she said it, but it didn't bother him too much. And when all of his new classmates started calling him Jesse, he decided not to tell them it was any different. Besides, he liked the sound of his new name. So from that time on he was Jesse.

Jesse Owens.

Devon Hind and Kate Bergstresser

Another change that came to the Owens household was getting paid at the end of each week. That never happened on the farm. Jesse's mama wasted no time finding houses to clean and laundry to wash. She was paid thirty cents an hour and glad to get it. The sisters also became maids, working for only a nickel less. The brothers found part-time work unloading boxcars, being janitors, or anything else that was available.

Even Jesse worked when he had the chance. He could be found some days delivering groceries while other times he might help sweep out the cobbler's shop. He worked in a greenhouse too. Anything Jesse could find that would pay a few pennies was fine with him. In no time, he was earning up to a dollar a week.

Henry Owens was the only family member who struggled to find a job. The difficult sharecropping life had made this skinny man with wrinkled, leathery skin look much older than his age. Even the most simple jobs usually required that he could read or write, but he could do neither.

No one wanted to hire him.

He spent many more hours looking for work than he did working. And when he did find a little part-time job, he wasn't paid much for it. In fact, the only one who made less money than him was Jesse.

Jesse Owens: World's Fastest Human

Every member of the family pooled their wages to help buy food and pay the rent. Soon there was enough money left for everyone to own three shirts instead of two. They could afford to eat meat once a week instead of once a month. For the first time, the Owens family had furniture that they didn't make themselves and the Christmas finally came when they bought a real Christmas tree with ornaments, not a scraggly one covered in socks and Mr. Clannon's trash.

Cleveland was good to everyone in the Owens family except Henry.

Henry Owens longed for those days when he had stood behind the plow, sweat stinging his eyes, smelling the freshly turned Alabama soil.

Year after year, Jesse's father searched for regular work and year after year he never found it. It pained him to know that he couldn't support his own family. But he never complained.

Henry did not dislike everything about his new home. He was pleased to see his family doing well in the city. They were happy going to work even though the labor was tough and the pay was little. Because Henry had taught his children how to work hard on the farm in Oakville, the part-time jobs soon turned into full-time employment. And he could see that Jesse was always eager to go to school. He thought back to those nine-mile family walks to church when his youngest child always told everyone about his dreams of going to college one day.

He could see that Jesse's dreams were still alive.

It was in grade school that Jesse met two people who would change his future. The first was Minnie Ruth Solomon. When he saw her, it was as if nothing else existed in the world except for her. All he could see was a little angel with beautiful brown skin. She smiled and he melted.

Jesse rubbed his damp palms on his pants, drew a deep breath and gathered the courage to talk to his new classmate that everyone called Ruth. Her family had just moved north from Georgia to escape the sharecropping life, just like Jesse's family! He had something in common with her. It was the key to making friends with her. It turned out to be a friendship that would last their entire lives.

Ruth seemed perfect to Jesse. He knew that something about her was different than anyone else he had ever known.

Many people looked down on families like Jesse's or Ruth's because of the color of their skin or because they lived in the poorer section of town. When people would say mean or hurtful things, Ruth always stood confident. She always looked on the bright side of things. The way she acted attracted Jesse to Ruth.

Jesse fell in love with Ruth just a little bit the first time they ever talked, and a little more every time after that. And when he felt like he could not love her any more, Jesse asked Ruth to marry him. She said that she would, even though they were only in the fourth grade.

Charles Riley taught Jesse physical education at Bolton Elementary. Mr. Riley was a coach from the neighboring high school who came over to the elementary school to help out.

He was a man of few words. Most of the time he communicated with the whistle that he kept around his neck. His index finger pointed to and fro when he wanted something done.

His quiet stone-faced manner earned the respect of his young students, but they were also intimidated because they were never sure what he was thinking. He usually leaned against whatever was available and held his whistle to his lips, always ready, just in case he needed to use it. He watched the activities of his students like a cat about to pounce on its prey. When he would motion for one of the boys to come over to him, they were usually nervous because they didn't want to meet up with his infamous paddle that they had heard about but had never actually seen.

For some time Jesse felt like this teacher's eyes had been burning a hole through him. It seemed like every time Jesse glanced in the teacher's direction he was looking straight at him. Jesse stayed on his best behavior. But one day it finally happened.

Just as school was letting out Jesse felt someone tap on his shoulder. He turned around to face his physical education teacher only one step away. Jesse's beaming smile vanished. He thought he might faint right there. His stomach churned and his face flushed.

Jesse nervously cleared his throat. A weak, "Yes sir?" was all he managed to say as worried wrinkles creased his forehead.

His mind started replaying every action of the school day.

What have I done wrong? was all Jesse could think.

Rise and Shine

"YOUNG MAN, I'M THE TRACK COACH at the high school," said Coach Riley, staring down at Jesse. "How would you like to be on our team in a few years?"

Jesse's nervous stomach that was making him feel like vomiting suddenly changed to butterflies. A tingle started in his shoulders and ran down the back of his arms and up the back of his neck. Hidden goose bumps had formed. Shocked by the question and trying to hide the excitement that had taken over his body, Jesse shuffled his feet, glanced quickly over his shoulder and asked, "You want me?"

Jesse couldn't understand why he had been singled out from the rest of his classmates. Though one of the tallest boys, Jesse certainly was not the fastest. He looked much skinnier and sicklier than the others too. However, the quiet Coach Riley could see beyond physical appearance. He noticed important things that others did not.

Charles Riley could watch children playing a game of kickball and know within minutes who he wanted on his future track teams. He noticed the person who was always intent on winning the game.

They were the ones who made a little grunt noise when they kicked the ball as hard as they could. They put every ounce of effort into the race to first base, never jogging or slowing down even when it was obvious that they would not arrive ahead of the ball. Coach Riley noticed whose shoulders slumped and whose demeanor changed when they were "out" instead of "safe."

The ones who caught Coach Riley's eye kept telling their teammates, "You can do it! Don't give up!" even when the odds of victory were stacked against their team. Though hidden in the crowd to most onlookers, certain students stuck out like sparkling diamonds in a pool of mud to the experienced coach.

Spindly Jesse Owens caught Coach Riley's keen eye months earlier. This fifth grader had the characteristics of all his past champions. Now he would find out if young Jesse was willing to work long enough and hard enough to be a success.

"That's right. Would you like to be on the track team in a few years?" Coach Riley repeated.

"Why, yes sir, I would," Jesse blurted.

"Then you'll need to start now. You'll need to do extra. Are you willing to work every day after school for an hour and a half to get better?"

"Why, yes sir, I would," Jesse stated again, shaking his head up and down to make sure he was understood.

The coach was not surprised by Jesse's enthusiastic response. He did not misjudge a person's character often.

"Good," he said. "Then I'll see you every day after school, starting tomorrow."

With that short conversation over, Coach Riley turned and walked away. Jesse could hardly contain his excitement.

The track coach wants me! was all he could think about as he raced off to his after-school job.

Suddenly, Jesse was in a panic. "Oh, no!" he said out loud to himself as he turned to run back to school. He had to find Coach Riley, and fast. Jesse ran back, his eyes scanning the landscape. When he turned a corner and saw the coach talking to some of his older athletes, he sped up and called out, "Coach Riley!"

The man in his fifties, who leaned a little forward when he walked, slowly turned around. Words spewed from Jesse's mouth even before he came to a complete stop. "I can't come to practice after school tomorrow!"

With eyebrows raised, the coach asked, "Why not?"

"I have to work after school. Every day I deliver groceries and sometimes I help at the cobbler's shop or greenhouse."

Coach Riley brought his hand to his chin, cocked his head to the side a little bit and stared off into the distance at nothing in particular. Finally he lowered his hand and looked back at Jesse.

"No problem," he said. "We'll meet before school then. Can you do that?"

"Yes, sir. Thank you, sir."

"I'll see you in the morning then. Two hours before school starts. That will give you some time to wash up. Every morning before school, right over there at the field house."

"Yes, sir!" Jesse replied as a smile overtook his worried expression. He turned around and hurried off toward his job once again. Each step he took got faster and faster as his excitement grew.

A smile rose slowly across Coach Riley's face and a sparkle filled his eyes as he watched the silhouette of his new protégé get smaller and smaller in the distance. He had thought that Jesse Owens was different from the rest. Now, he was certain of it.

He turned back to the athletes he was counseling and said, "He's going to be a good one some day." The runners turned to look at Jesse, not noticing anything special. They looked at each other with raised eyebrows and shrugged their shoulders.

The next day Jesse awoke before the sun was up, as excited as he was the morning of his fifth birthday. He was dressed and heading quickly out the door to Fairmont High School's field house when his mother opened her bedroom door and whispered, "Don't you need to eat some breakfast first?"

Jesse smiled at her, shook his head *no* and continued on his way.

"Work hard," Mama whispered, though Jesse was already too far down the front steps to hear her. A proud smile eased across her face. She knew that her son was much like her, determined to achieve more in life than most of the others that lived in their ghetto neighborhood.

Coach Riley stood waiting at school as Jesse came jogging around the corner.

"You're early." There was a pause. "I like that," he said.

For the next hour and a half, Jesse jumped,

stretched, ran and listened.

"Rome wasn't built in a day, Jesse. We're not looking for quick results. Just think of it like we're training for four weeks from next Friday. Be patient. If you trust me and do what I tell you, the hard work will pay off one day."

The beads of sweat collected in Jesse's eyebrows and dripped to the ground as he sat wide-eyed and cross-legged on the grass. He couldn't remember a time in his life that had been this much fun.

"There will be mornings, Jesse, when getting up early to come here will be much tougher than it was this morning. Your sore muscles and heavy eyelids will try to convince you to roll over and go back to sleep. Jesse..." Coach Riley paused, staring deep into Jesse's eyes, "champions put their feet on the floor and start moving. Never roll over, Jesse. I'll be here waiting for you."

With that said, Coach Riley reached out his hand to help Jesse to his feet. They walked slowly, side by side, to a paper bag that had been sitting by the field house wall. The coach leaned over, put his hand in the package and pulled out a bagel. He poured a large cup of water and handed both to Jesse. "Here," he said. "I figured you left before eating this morning."

Jesse Owens: World's Fastest Human

For the next three years the routine changed very little. Jesse's passion for running always consumed his thoughts. He never rolled over to go back to sleep, even during the cold winter months when the urge was great.

And Coach Riley was always there waiting for him with a welcoming smile, an encouraging word and, many times, a small bit of breakfast.

Devon Hind and Kate Bergstresser

Horses Don't Lie

MORE THAN TWO YEARS PASSED before Jesse entered his first track competition.

Jesse always knew his day would come. Still, the waiting and training had not been easy.

Jesse's body had grown stronger with the training.

He was so excited about finally getting to compete, he could hardly wait for the gun to go off.

Jesse was entered in the 440 yard dash, one-quarter of a mile. He did not understand why he was not running the shorter 100 or 220 yard dashes. But Coach Riley was testing more than Jesse's speed at this first race. He was testing Jesse's character.

Coach Riley wanted to know how determined Jesse would be in the final 180 yards. That is the point in the race when the muscles start to scream, "Slow down!" or "STOP!" Every 440 yard racer experiences it. Many will do what the muscles are demanding and give in to the pain and slow down. But the champion overcomes the cry of the muscles. He fights through

Jesse Owens: World's Fastest Human

the pain and pushes himself harder and harder, beyond what others think is possible.

Jesse was nervous. Coach Riley told him to relax and have fun, but even his words of wisdom could not settle the butterflies in Jesse's stomach. He looked at his competitors. Most of them were older and more experienced than he was. Still, Jesse was sure that he would win.

Each racer walked to his starting position on the cinder track. Each one looked around at the other runners and took deep breaths to settle his nerves. Some flailed their arms to stretch one last time, and most of them hopped up and down slightly to release some nervous energy. Finally, the starter raised the starting pistol and slowly said, "Set..."

Jesse looked straight down at the track in front of him. *You've got to win, Jesse. This is what you've been working so hard for. No one could have worked harder than you have,* Jesse thought to himself. *You will win.*

Pow!

The gun sounded and each racer took off at full speed. Jesse was in the lead after 100 yards. His legs churned as fast as he dared allow them to at this point in the race. He could hear footsteps of the runners behind him getting closer and closer. When he felt their presence over his shoulder, he burst ahead to keep them from passing. He was hoping they would get discouraged and give up. But they didn't get discouraged, and Jesse's legs were getting weaker.

Two of his opponents came up beside him and Jesse glanced at them. The dismayed look on his face seemed to say, *What do you think you're doing? I'm supposed to win this race!* Jesse did not have a burst of speed this time. They continued to ease past him and Jesse knew before the race was over that he would not win. He did not place third either. Jesse's disappointment showed before reaching the finish line when he eased up slightly. In that one short moment, another racer passed him. Jesse finished fourth.

Jesse had trained for more than two years to win and it was hard for him to accept defeat.

It did not matter to Jesse that his opponents were older and more experienced. He had convinced himself that he would win and the shock of this defeat hurt really bad.

Before the race Jesse had envisioned a crowd of his teammates running up to the finish line to excitedly congratulate him. He had also envisioned Coach Riley with a big smile stretched across his face that said, *That's my boy! Great job!*

It did not happen.

Jesse Owens: World's Fastest Human

Some teammates told Jesse, "Good try" and "Way to go," but he could tell they weren't any more excited than he was about the way his race had turned out.

Coach Riley was not standing there with a big smile either. In fact, he did not even go up to Jesse after the race. And Jesse could not find the courage to face his coach for a half hour. When he did muster the courage, Coach Riley was by himself setting up hurdles for the next race.

Jesse went and stood next to his coach waiting for him to say something. But he didn't.

Jesse finally broke the silence. "I thought I'd win. Why didn't I?" Jesse asked.

Turning to Jesse with a smile he finally answered, "Because you tried to stare them down instead of run them down, Jesse."

"I don't get it," he replied. "What does that mean?"

"I think you'll understand better if I show you rather than tell you. Are you busy Sunday afternoon?"

"No, sir. I hafta work in the mornin', but the rest o' the day is all mine."

"Good. I'm going to take you to see some of the best runners in the world. Be ready at one o'clock. I'll pick you up."

Jesse's spirits lifted immediately when he heard that. *The best runners in the world...WOW! I didn't even know that they were gonna be in town,* Jesse thought. *This is gonna be great!*

Coach Riley showed up right on time Sunday afternoon in his old car. He drove without saying a word, enjoying the scenery outside and occasionally giving Jesse a quick glance and a smile.

The excitement welling up in Jesse could not be contained any longer. "How much further?" Jesse asked after they had been driving for quite a while.

"Far enough," was Coach Riley's reply.

They drove for what seemed to Jesse like hours when they finally reached their destination. There were lots of other cars parked at this place, but Jesse was still not sure where he was. After Coach Riley paid for their tickets, they went inside the gate and through a building that did not have a roof. Jesse finally realized where they were. They were at the horse races!

Coach Riley marched Jesse to the fence so they could be as close to the horses as possible. "Watch these horses run," the coach said. "They run like no man can. Keep your eye on the ones that are in the lead at the finish. Watch their faces and watch how their body moves."

One race after another the two of them stood watching the races without saying a word. Jesse watched intently and learned. He studied the winning horse of every race.

When the races were finished, Coach Riley asked, "What did you learn?"

Jesse thought for a second and said, "Well...the horses in the lead never looked like they were trying very hard. You know that they had to be, but it didn't look like it. They were relaxed, effortless."

"And what did you see on their faces?"

"I'm not sure. I couldn't tell anything about their faces."

"Exactly, my boy! Horses don't lie. You couldn't tell anything about their faces because they weren't trying to tell you anything with them. They weren't trying to stare the other horses down. They're not actors. They're runners." Coach Riley paused, but soon realized by the quizzical look on Jesse's face that he needed some more explanation. "That's what your problem was the other day. You were trying to stare your opponent down. You were wasting your energy acting. Acting has never won a race. You need to focus all of your energy into your running, not into acting. Do you know why all of the best horses make it look easy out there? Because all of the determination is on the inside where no one can see it. They don't need to act."

Not another word was spoken the rest of the ride

home. Jesse let all of the images of those horses burn into his mind. He could see the determination and confidence with each of their graceful steps. He replayed Coach Riley's words over and over in his mind. He imagined what inner strength champions must have to make themselves the best.

One of the most valuable lessons Jesse ever learned came after a defeat rather than victory. Because he lost his first race, he learned what champions are made of.

He decided right then that he wanted to be a champion.

And for the rest of his life he never raced again without thinking of those horses.

Breaking Through the Barrier

"RUN FASTER AND RELAXED!" Coach Riley yelled out as Jesse circled the track during practice. "Feel the power in your steps... On your toes... That's right... Pretend the track is on fire... Light on your feet... Concentrate on your form... Relax!... Relax!... Relax!"

Coach Riley clicked the stopwatch as Jesse passed the finish line before slowing to a stop. The coach walked over to his hunched-over athlete and patted him on the shoulder. "Great job. Let's do it again. I know it's starting to hurt. This is when you have to really concentrate to relax. Don't tense up. Just relax...like the horses."

Jesse stayed hunched over with his hands on his knees, his chest moving in and out rapidly to keep pace with his heavy breathing. He turned his head slightly to the left, looking up to make quick eye contact with his coach. He shook his head *yes* to let his coach know he had heard him.

"Come on... Let's go... On the line. I don't want you to have too much rest or it won't do you any good," the coach said.

Jesse straightened up and swaggered to the starting line. Without saying a word, he stood ready to run again. His breathing was still heavy.

"Go," said Coach Riley as he clicked his watch. Jesse accelerated away from his coach. The words again rang out across the track, "Remember to relax... relax... relax... That's it... Great job... Keep it up... relax!" The coach stood silently gazing as Jesse finished his lap.

"Can you do one more?"

Jesse looked at his coach with that "Are you crazy?" look and shook his head *no*.

"I thought that's what you'd say," said Coach Riley as a big smile swept across his face. Jesse's sweat-drenched face displayed a relieved look as he thought practice was finally over.

Coach Riley then added with a chuckle, "Sure you can... One more... Let's go... On the line... You can do it... Last one... I promise."

Knowing it was useless to argue, Jesse walked slowly back to the starting line. His breathing was even heavier than it was the last time he stood at this spot only minutes earlier.

"Remember to relax... Go." Jesse sped off once again.

Jesse Owens was not afraid to work hard. He did it almost every day. It was something he had learned to do from as far back as he could remember. His parents had taught him well. He was determined to be the best runner in his school, his city, his country, and one day, the world. Jesse knew that it would take hard work to achieve his goals, so work hard he did.

And the hard work began to pay off. In junior high school, Jesse set a world record for students his age in the long jump by leaping 22 feet 11 3/4 inches. He set another record for students his age in the high jump by clearing 6 feet. He began to feel the taut finish-line string across his chest more and more often as he began to win races.

The sickly little boy from Oakville had worked his way into an athlete that opponents pointed to and whispered to each other, "That's him," as he arrived at competitions. But Coach Riley kept looking for something more out of Jesse.

In every person is a barrier. It is the place where we think that we can try no harder, achieve no more. We think we have nothing more to give. It takes great effort to even reach this point within ourselves where the barrier exists. Few can even get there. Coach Riley knew about the barrier, and he knew that it really didn't exist at all. It is like a mirage that every person's mind has put there. This barrier, this mirage, is what keeps many people from reaching greatness. Coach Riley knew it was his job to take his athletes to this hidden barrier and then beyond it, unleashing the potential inside the greatest of champions.

In Jesse's first high school varsity competition, he ran the 220 yard dash against some of Cleveland's best runners. Even though he was the youngest runner there, Jesse was determined to win. He had thought about nothing else for weeks.

Jesse stood at the starting line thinking about the race horses and all that he had learned in the past year.

Whatever it takes, I'll do it, he thought.

Jesse was standing still, gathering his strength and will. He would not be an actor today. No one could see the determination welling up inside of him, but it was there.

"You can do it, Jesse. Give it all you've got." Coach Riley's words caused Jesse's blank stare to turn into a faint smile. Jesse gave a slight nod of his head, acknowledging that he had heard the coach's encouragement. He stood tall, took one last deep breath, shook his hands to release nervous energy and crouched into his starting position.

When the starting gun sounded, Jesse exploded into the lead. He could tell by the sound of the spiked shoes crunching on the cinder track that the other runners were not far behind him. *You've got to push yourself harder*, he said to himself as the sound of footsteps became fainter and fainter. *Harder... Harder... Keep pushing... You've got to win today, Jesse... Push hard all the way.*

It is not possible to run full speed for an entire 220 yard dash. After the first 50 yards or so, racers usually "stretch it out," saving some energy for a final burst of speed to the finish line. Jesse was holding nothing back in this race. He knew that his body was moving across the track faster than it ever had before and it felt good to be in the lead. He pressed toward the finish line, digging deep within himself to muster all the strength he had. But as he rounded the final turn, his lead began to dwindle and he could hear the footsteps getting louder and louder as they closed in on him.

Push harder, Jesse, his mind screamed. *You will not be defeated! Push harder!*

Four racers gradually moved alongside Jesse and eased past him. But Jesse would not be quitting on himself today.

Catch back up! Don't let them go! You must win today, Jesse! You must! Jesse fought through the pain he was feeling and began to dig deeper and deeper for the energy he needed. He was looking for the inner strength that once lifted him to his knees when he was dying at five years old. And he found it. Jesse's muscles were crying out in pain, but he ignored their pleadings for relief. He was fighting back this time. He would not be denied victory. Jesse began to close the gap of the four runners in front of him. One had fallen behind the other three and Jesse passed him. The other three were almost in his grasp. *Get them! Get them! Get them!* is all he could think as he inched closer to his goal. And then the race was over. He had finished fourth. He had not caught up in time.

Jesse passed the finish line but he did not slow down. Disappointment flooded Jesse's soul and something deep within would not let him slow until he had passed those three. He kept at full speed, even though he felt like a fool for doing it, moving like a train that could not be halted. But he had to stop sometime. The school-yard wall loomed ahead of him. Jesse finally eased his pace, but he still slammed into the wall, bruising his elbow. He didn't feel the pain in his elbow. The pain was too great deep down inside of him.

He had done all he could do and he still finished fourth. His whole body slumped as he lowered his head in despair and turned away from the infield in shame. He wanted to hide from the whole world.

"You did it! You did it!" a familiar voice was yelling. When Jesse looked up in the direction of the sound he saw his coach running toward him with the biggest smile on his face he had ever seen. Coach Riley was holding his watch with one hand to keep it from bouncing up into his face and holding his hat to his head with the other hand. It suddenly occurred to Jesse that he had never seen his coach run before.

"I know you think you lost today, Jesse, but you didn't! You didn't beat those three out there, but you beat a much bigger foe. And that's the important thing! In my eyes you won today, Jesse! You beat that foe that I've been telling you about for so long. And you didn't just beat him once, you beat him a hundred times out there. Even when the race was over, you beat him some more."

Coach Riley, usually a man of few words, was talking faster than Jesse had ever heard him talk before. The excited coach then lowered his voice, making sure no one else could hear him. He looked Jesse straight in the eyes and said, "And I'll tell you something else too. Something I've never told anyone else before. Ever. Tomorrow is a new day with new opportunities. And there's no guarantee that you'll beat your foe tomorrow. But if you'll race like you did today and beat him again and then again and then again, you'll go to the Olympics some day. But even if you're as fast as those winning race horses we saw, it won't do you any good unless you can race like you did today. You know who you beat, don't you?"

Jesse shook his head *yes*. He knew without a doubt that he had given every ounce of effort that he had within himself. He had not quit on himself this time. He had not been an actor. Jesse had broken through "the barrier."

Jesse learned a valuable lesson in those moments. He learned that the real competition was himself. There was no shame in finishing behind someone else if he had gone deep within himself and fought through the pain and not given up. The shame that he felt only moments earlier began to turn to pride as he realized the truth of Coach Riley's words. The pain of defeat began to turn to the exhilaration of victory as he recalled the excited words, "You did it! You did it!"

Jesse had not spoken a word. Coach Riley could control himself no longer and gave Jesse a big bear hug. "I'm proud of what you did today, Jesse."

As they turned back toward the track, Coach Riley

Jesse Owens: World's Fastest Human

put his arm around Jesse's shoulder and they walked to the infield where his teammates gave him sincere congratulations. Jesse felt good about what he had done. And even though it seemed impossible only moments earlier, Jesse knew at that moment that he would be in the Olympics some day.

Owens' high school track team. Jesse is sixth from the left on the front row.

Wedding Bells

TRACK AND FIELD was not the only interest of the teen-age Jesse Owens. By the time Jesse was 16 and Ruth Solomon was only 14, their relationship took a big step.

They decided to get married.

"Jesse, I'm scared," Ruth said as they sat in the back seat of their friend, David Albritton's borrowed car. David had offered to drive Jesse and Ruth to find someone who would marry them on this Saturday in 1930. "I just know my parents are gonna have it out on me when we get home. How am I supposed to tell them?" Ruth said in a quiet but frantic voice.

Jesse took her hand and looking into her eyes said, "Ruth, you were the first girl I ever loved and the only girl I ever will love. It's gonna be hard for both of us. This is a big choice we've made, but we'll get through it...one step at a time."

Ruth looked into Jesse's eyes and held his hand the whole way to Pennsylvania, a state that didn't require parents to sign papers for such young teenagers to marry. She was confident that everything would work out fine.

After driving for hours, stopping at several towns along the way, Jesse and Ruth had yet to find anyone who would marry such a young couple. Tension was growing until they finally stopped in Erie, where a justice of the peace agreed to marry them.

The time had come and there was no turning back. Both Jesse and Ruth were nervous as they approached the spot where they were to be named husband and wife. There were no wedding bells, no flowers and no confetti. No smiling audience to hug and congratulate them as they left the courthouse. Only David Albritton as their witness. As they walked into the future, arm in arm, none of that mattered. For that one blissful moment in time, the world was theirs. Neither of them said a word because nothing needed to be said. They were happy to be young and in love.

There was no honeymoon for these newlyweds. After paying for the justice of the peace and gas for the car, there was little money left for even a wedding meal. The three travelers had only enough money for a single hot dog which they cheerfully shared.

As they rode home, the reality of what they would face when they got there seemed engraved in the back of their minds. They suspected that their parents would not be as excited as they were. It was late at night when they arrived in Cleveland, so Jesse and David dropped Ruth off at her home, returned the borrowed car and then Jesse ran the ten miles back to his house where he met his upset mother. She wanted an explanation of where he had been.

Eventually Jesse and Ruth shared the truth of that adventurous Saturday with their parents. Ruth's father was furious. He vowed that his daughter would not be allowed to see Jesse again. This obviously put a strain on their relationship, but it was impossible to keep them separated forever. Two years later, on August 8, 1932, Ruth gave birth to their first of three daughters, Gloria Shirley. Ruth had to drop out of high school to take care of the baby. She went to work in a beauty parlor while living with her parents who would still not allow Jesse in their home. Because of this, Jesse could not do a lot of the things for his baby daughter that most fathers do.

Instead, he concentrated most of his energies into running.

A Dream Comes True

BY 1932, JESSE OWENS WAS KNOWN as one of Ohio's greatest athletes.

Though talented in several sports, Jesse gave up football and basketball because they demanded too much of his running time.

He led his East Technical High School track team to a state championship his sophomore year in 1931 and again the following year. Jesse was sometimes called a one-man team because he often scored over half of his team's points.

Jesse's dream of going to the Olympics did not come true in 1932. He qualified to attend the Olympic trials at Northwestern University in the 100 and 220 yard dashes, but he lost in the preliminaries to America's top sprinter of that year, Ralph Metcalfe. Metcalfe won a bronze medal in the 200 meters and a silver medal in the 100 meters behind another American, Eddie Tolan, in those Los Angeles Olympic Games.

Failing to reach his Olympic dream in 1932 caused Jesse to work even harder than before. He was determined to be the best in the world. It wasn't long after the Olympics ended that Jesse began gaining valuable experience against runners from other countries. Many Olympic runners toured the United States to run in different track meets. When they came to Cleveland, Jesse beat all of them in the 100 and 220 yard dashes. He also finished a close second to the Olympic gold medalist, Edward Gordon, in the long jump. He was only a junior in high school at the time.

Jesse's high school senior year proved to be even

A young Jesse with his high school track medals

more impressive. His classmates, most of them white, chose Jesse to be student body president. It was something that almost never happened. In those days, black people were almost never treated as equals by white people.

Jesse never lost a competition his final season. During the Ohio state championships, he broke the world high school record in the long jump, leaping 24 feet, 3 1/2 inches. It would remain the Ohio state championship record for 44 years.

The Owens' mailbox was filled with letters from colleges around the country asking Jesse to attend their university and compete for their track team. They offered to help pay his college bills or give him a high-paying job that didn't require much work. Some even hinted at benefits like cars or spending money. Jesse needed advice.

"I'm not sure what to do, Coach. I have all of these opportunities and I don't know where I should go to college. It's all so confusing to me."

"Why don't you come to my office on the last day of school," Coach Riley replied. "We'll discuss it when your season is over. Don't worry about it until then."

Only a few weeks later, in his final high school meet in June 1933, Jesse won four gold medals at the National Interscholastic Championships in Chicago. He was so spectacular that newspapers all over America printed stories about him. In the 100 yard dash, Jesse tied the world record of 9.4 seconds and in the 220 yard dash he set a new world record of 20.7 seconds. He added an additional six inches to his high school long jump world record. His 4 x 220 yard relay team also set a new meet record. Four events and four new records, three of them world records! It was even more impressive because Jesse's leg muscles ached from cramps the night before and he only had 20 minutes of rest between each event. Jesse Owens was on his way to becoming a superstar.

When Jesse returned home, he was honored with a victory parade. He sat in a convertible next to his father and mother as it weaved through cheering crowds in downtown Cleveland. Coach Riley followed in another open car.

Only 700 miles and eleven years separated the Owens from that little town of Oakville, Alabama, but it seemed a million miles and forever ago.

So much had been gained in the Owens' family by the move north, but much had been lost too. Like the long walks to and from church every Sunday so many years ago. Those special times the family spent together talking about hopes and dreams. Life had become so busy in Cleveland that special moments like those were only memories. And sadly, Sunday mornings meant less and less to Jesse and his family.

Jesse could see the broad smile beaming from his father's face as he so proudly waved to the cheering fans, but Jesse could also see a wilted spirit in the man who once labored in the fields from dawn to dusk to provide for his family. Even after eleven years, Henry Owens was still moving from part-time job to part-time job. And the proud spirit and the tall frame that had once belonged to Jesse's father wilted a little more each time he heard one of his bosses say, "You're not needed any more." It was difficult for Jesse to ignore.

How could any of the thousands who were cheering young Jesse know that behind his smiling face there were troubling thoughts. Memories of Oakville and the special things that had been left behind haunted Jesse. He knew his life was getting more hectic with each passing day. The demands for his time were increasing and the pressures to perform at high levels never went away. He felt like his life was spinning out of control and he longed to reel it back in, but he did not know how. Memories of Oakville and its simpler life did not appear so bad to him at that moment.

On his final day of high school, Jesse walked into

Devon Hind and Kate Bergstresser

Coach Riley's office for advice about college. Coach Riley was sitting at his desk reading his *Bible*. Whether the coach intended to or not, he had shown Jesse how to get his life under control. "Keep your priorities in order" was the clear message the coach had sent in that short moment. And when Coach Riley leaned forward to put his *Bible* on the desk, a piece of paper fell, slowly floating to the floor and landing at Jesse's feet.

Jesse picked the paper up and glanced to see what it was. It was the poem *Excelsior* by Longfellow. When Jesse offered it back, his coach said, "No, Jesse. It landed at your feet. Keep it. I know it by heart, anyway. Read it some day, when you feel the need."

Feel the need? Jesse thought to himself. *Why would I need to read that poem?* Jesse put the paper in his wallet. When his wallet wore out and he got a new one, the paper went in the new wallet. Wherever he went, Jesse carried that paper with him. And one day when he felt "the need," he would read it.

The athlete and his coach talked for a long time about the college offers. Some were further from home than others. Some had better track programs. Some had better teachers. Some offered to help pay for more of Jesse's education than others.

"Which of the scholarships should I take?" Jesse finally asked.

The reply was not what Jesse expected.

"None of them," Coach Riley said matter-of-factly. "I think you should pay your own way."

So that is what Jesse did. Coach Riley took Jesse to visit a few campuses during the summer and Jesse finally enrolled at Ohio State University. His dream of going to college was coming true.

Jesse graduated from high school in the middle of the Great Depression. It was a time in America when few people had jobs and little money. Not many high school graduates had the chance to go to college, especially black high school graduates.

Jesse was one of only a handful of black students who attended college in the United States during that Depression year of 1933. He asked the school to provide him with only one thing.

"If possible, could you find my dad a full-time job on campus if one comes available?" Jesse asked.

It took about a year, but a groundskeeper-maintenance position finally emerged and for the first time since leaving Oakville Henry Owens had a regular job.

Devon Hind and Kate Bergstresser

45 Minutes In History

"I'LL BE GOOD, RUTH. The track coach got me an easy job working a freight elevator at the State House in Columbus. There's not much to do on the night shift, so I'll be able to use that time to study. I won't be pumping gas like I did this summer. You take good care of Gloria while I'm away. I'm gonna send you some money when I get paid. We'll be together soon...forever...I promise."

Ruth's father was allowing the two teenagers to see each other now, even at his own house.

"I love you, Jesse. You better be good. I'll miss you."

With that, Jesse was off to college.

Ohio State University.

There was only one dormitory for men at Ohio State and blacks were not allowed to live there. Jesse moved into a house near the campus with other black athletes.

His first priority was his running career. But too much running and not enough studying caused Jesse's grades to drop. He was put on academic probation for his first spring semester and ordered to bring up his grades. East Technical High School had not prepared Jesse for the hard classes at Ohio State.

He seemed to always have a hard time in class.

But Jesse's track career flourished. He worked hard under his new coach, Larry Snyder. This coach, like Coach Riley, pressed Jesse to relax his running style even further and he taught Jesse new starting and jumping techniques.

Before running his first college race, Jesse was named to the Amateur Athletic Union's (AAU) All-American track team.

In those days, freshmen were not allowed to compete in varsity track meets, so Jesse ran in other competitions. In the Big Ten Freshman Outdoor Championship meet in Columbus, Ohio, he won the 100, 220 and long jump, setting new conference records in each one.

Jesse proved himself ready for varsity college competition in his first Big Ten Conference meet in February 1935 by winning three events and placing second in the 70-yard low hurdles. The highlight of his college career came a few months later at the Big Ten Championships in Ann Arbor, Michigan on May 25th, 1935.

It was a championship meet that Jesse's coach was not sure he should be in.

"No, Jesse. I'm not going to let you do it. You've had hot packs on your back for the past week from falling down those steps at school. I just don't think it would be a good idea for you to compete yet. You might get injured worse," Coach Snyder explained to Jesse just before the meet.

"Aw... please... Coach. You said if I felt okay that you'd let me. I can do it, Coach. Just let me try the 100. That's the first event. If it hurts too bad, I won't do any more. I'll be honest with you, Coach. I promise. Please, Coach. Just let me try. Please."

Coach Snyder shook his head as he stared at the ground listening to Jesse's pleadings. The room was silent except for the sounds of keys jingling as the coach nervously fidgeted with them in his pants pocket. On the other side of the door, Jesse's teammates held their breath as they listened intently for the coach's answer.

Coach Snyder pulled off his cap and ran his fingers through his hair. "If it hurts you at all, I'll be able to tell and I'll pull you out of the meet. Don't argue if I have to do it. I want you to run in this meet as badly as you want to do it. But...I'm not going to risk the rest of your career for this one meet. You hear me?"

Jesse could hardly contain his excitement. "Does that mean I'm in, Coach?"

"Just for the 100 right now. We'll decide after that about the rest of the meet. You understand?"

"Yes, sir. Thank you, sir. I'm gonna be okay, Coach. You'll see."

Coach Snyder still wasn't sure he was doing the right thing.

Outside the door, Jesse's teammates slapped each other on the back and jumped up and down as they scurried down the hall, afraid that Coach Snyder might hear their excitement and know that they had been eavesdropping.

When Jesse bent down at the 100 yard dash starting line to dig the holes for his feet in the cinder track, his back pain disappeared.

"Set," the starter announced.

Jesse stared at the cinders, listening intently for the sound of the gun so he could power down the track and prove to his coach that he was healthy enough to compete. When the gun sounded, he sped down the track and finished first. He had qualified for the next round of competition. His back still wasn't hurting.

"I feel fine, Coach. I can do the rest."

"Okay," his coach replied. "But if it starts to hurt, you better let me know."

During the finals, Jesse wore his maroon top with the gray letters OHIO sewn across the front. His shorts were white with maroon stripes down each side. The uniform was about to go with Jesse Owens into the history books.

In the finals of the 100 yard dash, Jesse tied his own world record of 9.4 seconds. He next raced in the 220 yard dash finals. He improved his best time by

Running for Ohio State University

four-tenths of a second, setting a new world record of 20.3 seconds. Only minutes later, he set another world record in the 220 yard low hurdles, running 22.6 seconds and finishing 10 yards ahead of second place. The fans cheered wildly. They had just witnessed three world records.

Jesse still had one event to go.

The long jump.

It was the last event of the day.

Jesse asked a friend, "Can you take this handkerchief and put it at the 26-foot mark next to the pit for me, please? I'm going for it today. I'm feeling incredible."

"You bet," his smiling friend replied, taking the white cloth and heading toward the sand. He placed it at the designated spot, then cupped his hands and yelled, "You can do it, Jesse!"

And he did.

On his first and only attempt that day, Jesse Owens jumped 8 1/4 inches beyond the handkerchief, setting another new world record that would not be broken for 25 years.

Autograph seekers, photographers, reporters and well-wishers crowded around the man who had rewritten the record books. From beginning to end, Jesse had broken three world records and tied another in just 45 minutes. So many people waited outside the dressing room door that Jesse decided to escape through a back window. He recognized an old Model T in the parking lot. "Hi, Pop," Jesse said to Coach Riley as he jumped into the familiar old Ford. "Those crowds are somethin', aren't they? Thanks for bein' here."

"I would've been upset if I missed this one Jesse," the aging coach replied.

There was a pause as the two of them stared into each other's eyes. During this short silence, the smiles on each of their faces began to grow larger and larger, evolving into a soft chuckle. *Pop*, as Jesse called him, shook his head slightly from side to side and added, "You're somethin', Jesse Owens. You...are...somethin'."

Both of them broke out into jubilant laughter as Coach Riley shuffled his hand on top of Jesse's head like a grandfather might do to his young grandson. They drove off together and the coach, always the advisor, suggested how Jesse should handle this new fame.

The next day, headlines around the world announced that, beyond a shadow of a doubt, "The Buckeye Bullet" had given the greatest single performance in track and field history, a fact that remains true to this day.

High and Low Times

JESSE OWENS DID NOT WIN every race in the summer track meets that followed his record-setting day in Ann Arbor.

After a meet in Los Angeles in June, a beautiful young woman hung on Jesse's arm and a picture of the two of them ended up in the Cleveland newspaper.

Ruth was not too happy about the picture or the article that was with it. She finally talked to Jesse by telephone on July 3 when he arrived in Lincoln, Nebraska for the AAU Championships. The next day Jesse did not win a race and right then he took a train back to Cleveland to see Ruth.

It had been five years since Jesse and Ruth made the trip to Erie, Pennsylvania to get married, but they did not have a marriage license to prove it. So, on July 5, 1935, in the Solomons' living room where Jesse had been banned for so long, the two of them were married again.

Once again there was no honeymoon. Jesse left the next day to run a series of races. He lost repeatedly to another star athlete, Eulace Peacock. The papers were starting to write that Eulace Peacock might be the sprinter going to the 1936 Olympics rather than Jesse. Jesse came back home to his family in Cleveland discouraged and tired. He pumped gas for the rest of the summer.

Even going back to college was a problem.

"Ruth, they said I'm off the team until I make better grades. I can't believe it. I'm the world record holder in six events and they say I can't compete for the team!"

Jesse was broken-hearted by the news he had received from Ohio State University officials in the fall of his junior year.

And something even further from home worried him too.

The 1936 Olympics were to be in Berlin, Germany. Adolf Hitler, the German leader, was already getting prepared for World War II. The United States government didn't approve of what Hitler was doing, and threatened to boycott the Berlin Olympics to show how upset our government was.

Jesse Owens: World's Fastest Human

"I can't believe it," Jesse told Ruth. "Everything I've been working for all of these years could disappear right in front of me! What am I gonna do?"

Ruth put her arms around Jesse and squeezed him tight. She rested her head on his chest and said, "You're going to study harder than you ever have before to get those grades where they need to be. As for the Olympics, it's out of your hands. Remember what Coach Riley taught you. Don't worry about the things that you can't control. Everything will work out, I'm sure."

Things did begin to work out.
Jesse studied. He studied hard.
His grades got better.
He was back on the team.
He had been training on his own, away from the team, for months. He was in the best shape of his life, ready to take on the world again.

Jesse had forty-two straight victories for Ohio State in 1936. He set a new world record in the 100 yard dash when he ran 9.3 seconds on May 16. He again won four Big Ten titles and followed that with four NCAA Championship titles.

AAU officials decided that the U.S. would not boycott the Berlin games. But Eulace Peacock, who hurt his hamstring muscle, was no longer America's hope for the Olympic games.

Now Jesse was America's sprint leader.

And lead he did. Jesse won the 100 and 200 meters and the long jump at the Olympic Trials in New York City in July 1936. He was going to the Olympics! He left for Berlin on the ship SS Manhattan three days later.

Just before he left, Jesse met the legendary baseball player Babe Ruth at a dinner honoring the Olympians.

"You gonna win at the Olympics, Jesse?" Babe Ruth asked.

"I'll try," Jesse modestly replied.

"Everybody tries," Babe responded. "I succeed.

"Why? Because I know I'm going to hit a home run just about every time I swing a bat," the Babe went on. "I'm surprised when I don't! Because I know it...the pitchers...they know it too. *Know* you will win!"

Jesse listened intently to Babe's advice. He would soon need it. It wouldn't be long until he was standing before a crowd of one-hundred-thousand screaming spectators, not even sure if he would qualify for the finals of his Olympic event.

Olympic Fears

JESSE WAS SO CLOSE to living his dream he could taste it.

Already, he was one of the special few with a chance to run in the world's biggest competition, the Olympics.

Now a new mission lay in front of Jesse that loomed greater than the nearby great Alps.

It was a new challenge greater than that of any other Olympian.

All Jesse had to do was read the newspapers to know just how tough his challenge was.

He read the papers. The stories made him determined not only to win his races, but also to prove something else to the rest of the world.

Jesse grew up in a world where all men were not treated equally. White people looked down on black people everywhere in America. People with dark-colored skin were treated as inferior and sometimes even less than human.

Jesse had seen the disrespect and cruelty during his life because of the color of his skin. Besides having to live off-campus at Ohio State University, he and his black teammates either had to order carry-out meals or eat at "black only" restaurants. They were forced to stay at "black only" hotels as well. Now Jesse had a golden opportunity to prove to the world that he and other persons of color were just as good as anyone else.

The 1936 Olympics were hosted by Germany, a country where racial prejudice was obvious. It was even encouraged by the German leader, Adolph Hitler. He believed that his tall, fair-skinned, blond, blue-eyed Aryan (a white-skinned German of non-Jewish descent) supermen were better and smarter than anyone else and should rule the world. He bragged that his athletes would prove that his master race was stronger, healthier and more athletic than the rest of the world. Hitler claimed that his athletes would prove their superiority when they competed against the American Olympic team.

Because of what Hitler said, reporters wrote a lot of stories about the American Olympic team. There were 19 black U.S. Olympic athletes that year. Ten of them were on the track team, including Jesse.

Jesse Owens: World's Fastest Human

Jesse already had set world records in several track events.

Hitler hated the black athletes.

He wanted his blond-haired, blue-eyed track stars to whip them.

He wanted it bad.

The German people didn't seem to feel the same way, though.

Jesse got to Berlin two weeks before the games began.

Everywhere he went the German people were friendly and nice to him. Everyone wanted his autograph and to pose with him for photographs. The Germans thought it was funny when Jesse used the few German words that he had learned for his trip to the Olympics. Crowds gathered around Jesse morning and night.

Ohio State track coach Larry Snyder was in the crowd that watched Jesse practice in Olympic Village one day. David Albritton, Jesse's high school and college teammate and friend, also was on the team as a high jumper. Coach Snyder was not one of the Olympic coaches. He just wanted to see the games and had paid his own way to Berlin. It was a good thing for Jesse that he did.

"Jesse," Coach Snyder called out and waved. Jesse came walking toward him. "What were those drills you were doing out there today?"

"The coaches are trying to teach me a new running style, Coach. They think that I'll run faster if I'll not be so relaxed. They want me to power down the track. They think I'm not giving it all I've got and I'll really win big with their style."

"What!?" Coach Snyder shrieked. "Less than two weeks before the most important races of your life and they want you to change the very thing that got you here? You wait here. I'm going to talk with them. Oh, yeah. Jesse, those don't look like your track shoes. Where are yours?"

Jesse dropped his head, a little embarrassed. "Oh, I lost mine at the Olympic trials. I'm not sure what happened to them, but I couldn't find them after the meet. These are some others I came up with."

"Well, how do they feel? Are they okay?" the coach asked.

"Not really. I liked my others much better. But these really aren't too bad."

"I'll see what I can do about those too," Coach Snyder replied as he walked off.

Snyder talked to Jesse's Olympic coaches about leaving his running style alone. Coach Riley and he

Jesse Owens: World's Fastest Human

had spent years perfecting Jesse's technique and it was that technique that helped Jesse become "the world's fastest human".

"After all," Coach Snyder concluded, "technique takes years to develop, not days."

Reluctantly, the new coaches agreed.

As for the track shoes, Coach Snyder spent days looking through the shops of Berlin until he found just the right pair.

Hitler had ruled Germany for only three years. In that short amount of time, however, the people who lived there were making more money than before Hitler took over and they were more proud of their country than they had been in a long time. Super highways, called *autobahns*, had been built. Airplanes and blimps, called *zeppelins*, were being mass produced. Young people were being taught to have strong minds and strong bodies. These youngsters took pride in their new leader and country. They were convinced that he could do no wrong.

But Hitler had already done very mean things to many people. After only a month as Germany's leader, he ordered fifty concentration camps to be built, then had thousands of people arrested and sent there as "enemies of the state." They were mostly Jews, Communists, Catholics, and other people who Hitler disliked. They lived in horrible conditions. Much of the world didn't seem to notice what Hitler was doing or was not aware of his behind-the-scenes schemes.

Hitler spent a lot of money to help Germany get ready for the Olympic Games. He intended to put on a big show for the rest of the world and he wanted everything to be impressive. The athletes found everything to be first class.

Hitler wanted his athletes to be impressive as well. That is why he had his Aryan supermen train in very special ways for the Berlin Olympic games.

Hitler bragged all the time about Germany and the German athletes. Every time he started bragging, the newspapermen from around the world would ask, "Who does Germany have that will beat Jesse Owens?"

Hitler didn't answer the question for months. But since the Olympics were about to begin, he finally told the world what it had been waiting to hear. Luz Long was the name and he would compete in the long jump.

Hitler guaranteed that Long, Germany's superstar, would win.

Jesse Owens had heard of Luz Long, but he did not know how good he was or what he looked like.

Jesse Owens: World's Fastest Human

He soon found out.

On August 1, 1936, the Olympic athletes from around the world marched into Olympic Stadium to the cheers of one-hundred-thousand spectators. As the athletes walked past Adolf Hitler, they gave the Olympic salute which was the arm stretched out to the right. For the Americans, this looked too much like the Nazi (Germany's political party) salute which was the arm stretched out in front of the body. Just to make sure no one thought that they were saluting their approval for the German leader and his political beliefs, the Americans put their hand over their heart. The German leadership and many of the German spectators didn't like what the American's did. But there was nothing they could do about it.

Jesse Owens peered through the crowd in search of Luz Long, Hitler's super athlete.

Suddenly his eyes landed on a perfect athletic specimen—tall and muscular and handsome—wearing a German uniform.

That has to be Luz Long, Jesse thought to himself.

He was right.

Jesse later said that Long was "a supreme example of Aryan perfection...one of those rare athletic happenings you come to recognize after years in competition—a perfectly proportioned body...stunningly com-

Devon Hind and Kate Bergstresser

pressed and honed by tens of thousands of obvious hours of sweat and determination." Jesse stood and stared at Luz Long.

He hated to admit it, but he was intimidated by the sight of his competition.

Jazze Owens!

JESSE DIDN'T HAVE TO WORRY about Luz Long for the first two days of Olympic competition.

August 2nd began the 100 meter dash races. It was a cool day with a steady drizzle falling. The cinder track became muddy. But that didn't slow down Jesse Owens. He breezed to victory in the first qualifying round, tying his world record of 10.3 seconds. And he even bettered that in the quarter-finals later that day by a tenth of a second. But because a breeze was blowing from behind him, his new record would not count.

When Jesse was through running for the day, he decided to watch his friends in the high jump where Cornelius Johnson and David Albritton finished first and second. Johnson soared 7 feet 6.5 inches for a new world record.

Adolph Hitler was not happy.

He congratulated all the Olympic medalists, except the black Americans. He refused to congratulate them. Olympic officials ordered him to greet all of the athletes or none at all. For the rest of the Olympic Games, Hitler greeted no one.

The 100 meter semi-finals and finals were the following day and the track was even muddier from heavy rains. Once again, Jesse Owens would not be denied. Wearing one inch spikes in his brown shoes and a white uniform with a red, white, and blue stripe running from his right shoulder to his left hip, #733 streaked to victory down the inside lane of the track in 10.3 seconds. Jesse had won his first Olympic gold medal. Ralph Metcalfe, the one who kept Jesse from qualifying for the 1932 Olympics, earned the silver medal. Again, the United States had a one-two finish.

Jesse salutes from victory platform after winning Olympic gold; Luz Long is at far right, behind Jesse

Jesse Owens: World's Fastest Human

Even though Hitler was not happy, German fans filled the stadium cheered when Jesse stood on top of the victory platform. Besides receiving the crowd's cheers, a laurel wreath was placed on Jesse's head, an oak tree sapling in his hand, and a gold medal around his neck. Tears of joy filled his eyes as he saluted the rising American flag. The hate that Hitler had spent years pounding into his countrymen was quickly being erased by the sharecropper's son from Oakville, Alabama.

August 4th brought more rain. Jesse easily made it through his qualifying round of the 200 meter race that morning.

The long jump qualifying was next. Jesse had to jump 24 feet 6 inches to advance to the finals that would be held later that afternoon. Like the other jumpers, he could try three times to make the distance. Jesse had jumped further than the qualifying mark in every track meet during the previous two years, so qualifying should not have been any problem. But it was.

"I can't believe I just did that!" Jesse said as he stood in his warm-up suit, shaking his head in disgust.

"Don't worry. You'll get it on your next one," a bystander encouraged.

Devon Hind and Kate Bergstresser

Jesse had sprinted down the runway in his sweat suit for what he thought was one last practice jump. But the judges counted it as an official jump. He was three inches short of the required distance. He had only two more tries.

Luz Long qualified easily for the finals on his first attempt. In fact, he broke the Olympic record.

Jesse could see Hitler's projected winner relaxed and having fun watching the other competitors.

Suddenly, sad, ugly thoughts crept into Jesse's mind. *What if Hitler's right? Maybe his Aryan race are supermen. This is Long's home turf and I'm so far from home. Maybe he's meant to win today.*

Stop thinking like that, Jesse! he screamed silently to himself. *Stop thinking like that! Stop thinking like that!*

Finally, Jesse cleared his head and got ready for his next jump. He re-measured his steps to make sure they were just right.

He stood on the runway rocking gently back and forth staring blankly at the sand pit a hundred feet away.

"Just qualify, Jesse. Just qualify," he nervously murmured to himself just before sprinting toward the sand pit.

"Foul!" shouted an official as Jesse landed in the

Jesse Owens: World's Fastest Human

sand.

Jesse's second jump would not count. His foot had gone past the take-off board.

Only one more try. Terror gripped his soul and news reporters swarmed him like bees.

"What's wrong...? What if...?" the reporters demanded. As confidently as he could, Jesse answered their questions until they finally left him alone.

One of the American reporters pointed out to Jesse, "Did you know Hitler walked out on you? Right before your first practice jump. Saw it myself. Hitler made some vow not to look at you in action. Crazy?"

When Jesse hesitantly looked toward Hitler's special front row seat, it was empty. It was Hitler's way of saying, "Jesse Owens is inferior."

And Jesse began to think that Hitler might not be so crazy after all.

Finally, Jesse stood on the runway for his third and final attempt. A battle raged in his mind.

You're not going to make it, Jesse.

I must. I must. Everyone's counting on me.

If you try too hard, you'll foul. If you don't try hard enough, you'll land short. It's over, Jesse. You've lost already.

I must find a way. I must.

One-hundred-thousand German fans and one

empty seat glared down on the lone black man on the runway. Jesse knew they wanted Luz Long, their German hero, to win. The loud speaker announced "Jesse Owens" for the third time. He stood staring, but not moving.

Jesse's time to jump was quickly running out before he would be disqualified. He couldn't delay jumping much longer. But fear held him back from that first step down the runway. He felt like vomiting.

Without warning, Jesse felt a hand on his shoulder.

"Jazze Owens. What has got your goat?"

Startled, Jesse looked up into two warm blue eyes. It was Luz Long.

A calm flowed through Jesse's once tense body.

"I think I know what is wrong with you. You are 100 percent when you jump. I the same. You cannot do halfway, but you are afraid you will fail again."

A smile spread over the worried expression on Jesse's face. "That's right," Jesse replied, nodding.

"I have answer," Long continued. "Same thing happen to me last year in Cologne."

Luz Long proceeded to quickly help Jesse re-measure his steps and suggested that he jump from six inches behind the take-off board, giving it all he had. That way Jesse could still give 100 per cent and not

Jesse Owens: World's Fastest Human

foul. Long even placed his towel at the spot from where Jesse should jump.

Confidence replaced the doubt that had nearly smothered Jesse moments earlier.

Jesse did not foul on his third attempt. In fact, he stayed in the air longer than any other Olympian had previously. When he landed, he had broken Long's short-lived record. Jesse had finally qualified for the finals and he immediately ran over to thank his new friend.

The rest of the afternoon found Jesse Owens and Luz Long in a heated battle for the Olympic gold medal.

But they were not enemies.

Because of Luz Long's ability to see past Jesse's skin color and Hitler's godless beliefs, the two were simply engaged in friendly competition. They encouraged and congratulated each other throughout the long jump finals. And the crowd did too.

After the first jump, Long trailed Jesse by one inch. On his second attempt, Long tied Jesse and his Olympic record of 25 feet 9 3/4 inches. On Jesse's second attempt he regained the lead and the record. He jumped 26 feet 1/2 inch.

Luz Long had only one more try.

Hitler had returned to his seat for the final competition. He sat nervously rocking back and forth as he intently watched Long make his final jump. But Long fouled, visibly upsetting Hitler.

Even though he already had captured the gold medal, Jesse took his third and final attempt. He mustered every bit of energy that he could find and leaped even further into the record books with a jump of 26 feet 5 1/4 inches.

Long was the first to congratulate him. He gave Jesse a hug in full view of the internally raging Adolf Hitler, then raised Jesse's arm, turned to the crowd, and shouted, "Jazze Owens! Jazze Owens!"

Some in the crowd began to respond. "Jazze Owens," they shouted.

Long began to shout even louder, encouraging everyone to join in.

Soon over one-hundred-thousand German fans in the stadium began to chant.

"Jazze Owens!

"Jazze Owens!

"Jazze Owens!"

It was deafening.

It was a moment like none other in Olympic history. The walls of racial hatred that Hitler had worked so hard to build had suddenly crashed down at his feet.

After the Gold

THE NEXT DAY, Jesse faced a new challenge. This one was from one of his own teammates in the 200 meter dash.

Mack Robinson, the brother of legendary baseball player Jackie Robinson, equaled Jesse's new Olympic record of 21.1 seconds in his semi-final heat.

Jesse faced the possibility that he would have to run the 200 meter finals faster than he ever had run it before. Faster than any human being had ever run it before.

Could he live up to such a challenge?

The world waited and watched.

In the finals, Jesse rocketed from the starting line and never looked back. He finished five yards in front of the second-place Robinson. He had set another new Olympic and world record of 20.7 seconds. And the Americans had another one-two finish.

Jesse still was not finished.

Devon Hind and Kate Bergstresser

On August 8th, he led teammates Ralph Metcalfe, Foy Draper and Frank Wycoff to victory in the 4 x 100 meter relay, a race in which each team member runs 100 meters, one right after the other. Whichever team's fourth runner crossed the finish line first would win.

Jesse's team won by fifteen meters and set another new Olympic and world record, running 39.8 seconds. The Germans finished third.

Hitler's dreams of showing the world his Aryan supremacy failed.

Jesse Owens was the first track and field athlete to ever win four Olympic gold medals at a single Olympics. He had broken Olympic records in all four events. He had become the most famous athlete in the world.

"Good-bye, Luz," Jesse said to his new friend as they embraced each other. "I promise that I'll write to you. You do the same. We'll meet again someday. We must! I love you, friend. You've helped me more than you'll ever know."

Jesse and Luz Long had spent most of their free time together since the long jump competition. Jesse regarded Luz Long as the closest friend he ever had. Though they kept in touch with letters, they never saw each other again.

Jesse Owens: World's Fastest Human

Poster-size photo of Jesse and Luz Long at Jesse Owens Museum in Oakville

Long died a few years later as a soldier fighting for Germany in World War II. He was killed in the desert of North Africa. The last letter he wrote before he died was to his close friend, Jesse Owens.

On that sad day when Jesse had to leave his friend when the Olympics ended, he wasn't headed home. Even though he deeply missed Ruth and his daughter, Amateur Athletic Union officials had different plans for the American Olympic track stars. To help pay for Olympic expenses, AAU officials planned a grueling schedule of meets around Europe to draw big crowds and lots of money. The athletes had to attend.

When Coach Snyder found out about the treatment of his Olympic athletes, he was mad. Jesse was exhausted from the Olympic competition and the additional meets drained him even further. After competing in the first five meets in different cities in Europe, Coach Snyder encouraged Jesse to come back to the United States to rest.

Jesse was in London at the time, and the next meet was in Stockholm, Sweden.

What should he do?

Go on to Stockholm as the AAU officials demanded?

Or take his old coach's advice: Go home and rest.

He badly needed the rest. He was ten pounds lighter than he was when the Olympics began. And he was tired. Bone tired.

Finally he decided.

He stayed in London.

The AAU officials were mad; so mad that they declared Jesse could never compete in amateur competition again.

The greatest track and field athlete in Olympic history had run the final race of his career in London the day before. Jesse Owens was being punished for wanting to go home and rest. He boarded the next ship departing for New York City.

A hero's welcome waited for Jesse when he arrived in New York. A boat ferried his family out to the ship before it even docked. Reporters flocked around him. Government leaders and wealthy businessmen threw big parties in his honor. They all had their pictures made with Jesse. And they all told Jesse how rich he would become. Many of them offered hints of high paying jobs.

Jesse and the mayor of New York rode in the mayor's convertible to the delight of thousands of fans that lined the streets, hoping to get a glimpse, or even touch him.

One fan threw a brown paper bag into Jesse's lap. He never saw who it was. When Jesse opened the bag, it was filled with thousands of dollars. The next day, Jesse sent $2,500 of the money to a Cleveland real estate salesman for a down payment on a house for his parents.

Life seemed to be going great for Jesse, but Ruth

Devon Hind and Kate Bergstresser

saw problems ahead.

After a few days, she told him, "Maybe I should go home before you, Jesse. These people really aren't our kind."

"You mean Negroes?" Jesse asked.

Shaking her head, Ruth replied, "You know I don't see it that way, Darling. Possibly I mean that they won't be there when the party's over."

"But the party's never going to be over," Jesse insisted. "And some of them will be around. Because I'll be working with them. You wouldn't believe some of the jobs that these millionaires have offered me."

Ruth gave Jesse an encouraging smile and hoped he was right. She went back to Cleveland the next day. Jesse stayed to decide who he wanted to work with.

He dialed the telephone numbers of the millionaires who had promised big things. "He's out of the office at the moment," Jesse was told. "He'll have to call you later Mr. Owens," was what Jesse heard most.

No one ever returned the calls. And no one ever seemed to be in the office. When Jesse would finally catch up with one of these big shots, they would beat around the bush and give him more empty promises.

Finally, what was left of the money in the brown bag ran out. The parties stopped. No one gave Jesse a job.

Jesse Owens: World's Fastest Human

He returned to Cleveland where the parties and parades started all over again. But that ended soon enough too and when the celebrating was over, this man who could not go anywhere without someone asking for his autograph was still without a job.

Jesse finally took the only job that he could find. He became a playground instructor for $28 per week. Only one year from graduating college, Jesse decided not to go back to school. Right then, he had to feed his growing family. It wasn't long before Beverly would be born, followed by her sister, Marlene.

Weeks later, two men sat in Jesse's living room explaining about the professional Negro baseball league. They wanted Jesse to help them promote the league.

A better job at last. The playground job was fun and exciting, but the pay was bad.

Jesse was getting excited until they said, "Oh, no. We don't want you to play in the league. We want you to race a horse in a 100 yard dash before the game. We know that lots of people will pay to see that."

Jesse was humiliated and asked the two men to leave.

"Let us know if you change your mind," they offered.

Devon Hind and Kate Bergstresser

"I won't change my mind," Jesse replied. Out of courtesy he took their business card and placed it next to his four gold medals.

Jesse was at the lowest point of his life that night. It had only been a few months since the highlight of his life when he had stood listening to the cheering crowd yell, "Jazze Owens! Jazze Owens!"

Where, Jesse wondered, *did those four gold medals get me?*

Epilogue

JESSE SOON SWALLOWED HIS PRIDE and accepted the promoters' offer to race horses before baseball games. He needed the money. He had to provide for his family and continue making payments on his parents' new home.

Racing those horses was humiliating for Jesse, but it paid well. He took advantage of other job opportuni-

Jesse racing horses; humiliating but it paid well

ties that came along too.

Jesse traveled the country making campaign speeches for the 1936 Republican presidential candidate, Alf Landon. But the Democrat, Franklin D. Roosevelt, won the election.

Even though he couldn't sing or play an instrument, Jesse became the leader of a black band that played in nightclubs across America. He organized a professional black basketball team and a traveling softball team as well. None of these adventures lasted very long.

Two men made Jesse another offer that he couldn't refuse. They wanted to use his name to start a chain of cleaning stores, "The Jesse Owens Cleaners." All he had to do was sit back and get paid. They would do all of the work.

What a deal! Jesse partnered with the men and the money rolled in. He had quit racing horses by then. He paid off the mortgage on his parents' house and bought one for himself. He treated Ruth to nice things and they had a car of their own. He went back to college. The cleaning stores were spreading like wildfire. Jesse was again feeling on top of the world. But he didn't stay there long.

Jesse's business partners skipped town and left Jesse with a debt of $114,000.00. All of the bills were in Jesse's name. He didn't know how he would ever be able to pay that much money back, but he offered the bank fifty dollars a week until the debt was paid in full. It would take almost fifty years to clear the debt at that rate. Jesse thought the banker might laugh at him or call the police to have him arrested when he explained his idea. But to Jesse's surprise, the banker accepted the offer.

Jesse couldn't leave the banker's office without asking, "Why...why are you doing this...trusting me?"

"It all comes down to whether we think you're honest or not..." the banker replied. "...whether we think you'll pay us back or not. It doesn't really matter how long it will take. We think you're a good bet to pay it back. Jesse, there's one more thing. I'm half Jewish. How could I ever not trust the man who beat Hitler?"

If there's one thing that Jesse Owens knew how to do, it was work hard. He worked as much as he could, determined to pay back the money he owed in much less time than fifty years.

When America entered World War II after the bombing of Pearl Harbor on December 7, 1941, Jesse wanted to do his part in the war effort. When Jesse offered to serve his country, he was flown to Washington D. C. where he was introduced to President

Roosevelt.

"I think you can help move us toward victory," the president told Jesse.

Jesse was hired to organize exercise programs at black schools and community centers across the country. Then he was asked "to supervise the hiring of Negroes for the wartime effort in the Ford Motor Plant in Detroit." The assembly lines were being turned into factories to make wartime machinery.

On the Friday before the Germans surrendered in 1945, Jesse made his final payment to the bank. His hard work had paid off. He was out of debt.

For the next twenty years, Jesse worked like no other. He was in demand as a speaker and a public relations guest all around the world. It was not uncommon for him to work twenty-hour days, never slowing down. He traveled for two, three, four weeks at a time without seeing his family. When he would go home, his stays were short.

Jesse loved his family and showered them with gifts from his travels. But his three girls grew up and he hardly knew them. Ruth never complained though she longed for her husband to be home more often.

Jesse felt guilty about the schedule he kept. He knew he needed to be home more. But he didn't know how to break the cycle he was in. So many organizations asked for his help. And he didn't know how to tell them "no."

In September 1956, Jesse's oldest daughter, Gloria, told him that she was getting married. Two days later Jesse made good on his promise to Ruth to quit traveling so much.

"I want to be home more with my family," Jesse admitted.

Jesse canceled most of his plans and found work in their hometown of Chicago. He still worked the twenty-hour days sometimes. But he slept in his own bed at night. He was with his family more often.

In 1965, troubles began piling up again for Jesse.

His bad habit of smoking cigarettes began to take its toll and his aging body was feeling the stress from all those long workdays. He developed ulcers in his intestines. He almost died of pneumonia. Doctors operated on him for paralyzing back pain. Fortunately, his health improved. But his business took a turn for the worse.

The United States government accused Jesse of not paying taxes. The person in Jesse's company who was responsible for tending to his taxes had not done so in four years.

Jesse didn't realize it. He owed the government a

lot of money. Much more than the $114,000.00 he owed from the dry cleaning business debts.

Jesse had always been a spender and not a saver. He did not have the money to pay his tax debt. He could be sentenced by a judge to spend the rest of his life in prison.

Newspapers ran stories about Jesse's tax problems. Almost everyone treated Jesse like a criminal before he ever went to court. His business clients deserted him first. Then others. Very few remained loyal to him except for his family.

Henry and Emma Owens had always taught their son to be honest. He continued to live by their advice. Jesse stood alone facing the judge.

"I never tried to cheat anyone in my life, your honor—except possibly Jesse Owens—so...help...me...God." That is all he said. No excuses. No begging for mercy. Only the simple truth.

The judge replied, "Never has a defendant stood before the court but what I haven't taken a look at his record. I hope when I get up above—if I get there—and Saint Peter looks down and finds some of my misdoings, he will at least take a look at the other side of the ledger and see if there isn't something to my credit. I've looked at the credit side of your record. I've seen enough."

Jesse Owens: World's Fastest Human

The verdict? Jesse had to pay everything that he owed, but the government trusted him to do it. He was free to go.

When Jesse made it outside onto the courthouse steps, he saw a blind man with a cup in his hand. He pulled out his wallet, but it was empty. He went to the special pocket where he kept his emergency twenty dollar bill and another piece of worn out, wrinkled paper. He put his last twenty dollars in the cup.

Jesse looked at the folded piece of paper. It was the one that Coach Riley had given him thirty-five years earlier.

"Read it when you have the need," his coach had suggested a lifetime ago.

For the first time ever,

Jesse, in his olympics uniform, with his high school coach, Charles Riley

Devon Hind and Kate Bergstresser

Jesse in later years, working with young people

Jesse unfolded the paper and read the poem *Excelsior*. And he cried.

His mind wandered back to the inside of Coach Riley's office those many years ago. The scene in his mind was as fresh as if it had been yesterday. Jesse was walking through the office door. Without saying a word the coach had communicated by his example. "Keep your priorities in order, Jesse. Keep your priorities in order."

Until dying of lung cancer in 1980, he tried to do just that.

Jesse Owens never found it in himself to slow down. It was not in his nature. After all, running is what made him tick. But along life's pathway, he was always encouraging the downtrodden and helping them to rise up. He assisted the disadvantaged at every opportunity. He did his best to meet the needs of those he encountered.

Ruth, his children, and eventually his grandchildren didn't always get to spend a lot of time with the forever busy Jesse Owens. But they realized all the good that he was doing throughout the world. His family loved and appreciated him as he was.

Jesse experienced the lowest of the valleys and the highest of the mountain tops during his lifetime. He will always be remembered for his hard work, his unprecedented athletic accomplishments, his honesty and his gentle, giving spirit. He loved life and he lived it to the fullest.

Devon Hind and Kate Bergstresser
Jesse Owens

1913 Born September 12, in Oakville, Alabama (Lawrence County)

1919 Moves to Cleveland, Ohio (The year of this move is unknown. Researchers place the date of the movebetween 1919 and 1922. The authors of this book use 1919 because it is the date that Jesse Owens used in his autobiography. However, the 1922 date would better explain why Jesse was much older than others in his first grade class.)

1927 Enrolls at Fairmont Junior High School

1928 Breaks junior high world long jump and high jump records

1930 Marries Minnie Ruth Solomon in Erie, Pennsylvania
Enrolls at East Technical High School

1932 Runs in 100 meter Olympic trials but loses to Ralph Metcalfe

1933 Breaks high school long jump world record

Jesse Owens: World's Fastest Human

Ties world record in 100-yard dash
Breaks world record in 220-yard dash
Victory parade held in Jesse's honor in Cleveland, Ohio
Enrolls at Ohio State University

1934 Named Amateur Athletic Union All-American Track Athlete before running a single college race
Set Big 10 freshman conference records in 100 yard dash, 220 yard dash and long jump

1935 Breaks three world records and ties a fourth at the Big 10 Championships in Ann Arbor, Michigan in a 45 minute time span
July 5th, Marries Ruth Solomon again to legalize marriage

1936 Undefeated in 42 consecutive competitions for Ohio State University
Wins four gold medals at the Olympics in Berlin, Germany
Declared ineligible for amateur competition by the AAU
Employed as playground instructor for underprivileged youth for $28/week

Devon Hind and Kate Bergstresser

1937 Races horses at baseball games, bandleader, owner of a basketball team

Partnership in a dry cleaning business

1940 Returns to Ohio State University to pursue college degree, but does not graduate

1941 In charge of national physical fitness program for the U.S. government

1943 Works at Ford Motor Company to help wartime efforts

1949 Moves to Chicago and forms public relations company

1950 Named by the Associated Press as the greatest track and field athlete in history

Appointed head of the Illinois Athletic and Youth Commission

1951 Asked to return to Olympic Stadium in Berlin where he is welcomed with open arms; runs around the track to the cheers of the crowd once again

1955 Named America's Ambassador of Sports by

Jesse Owens: World's Fastest Human

President Eisenhower; tours the world promoting amateur programs

1956 Named President Eisenhower's personal representative to 1956 Melbourne, Australia, Olympics

1965 Named the running coach for New York Mets baseball team

1970 Inducted into Alabama Sports Hall of Fame

1972 Receives honorary Doctor of Athletic Arts from Ohio State University

1973 Awarded Theodore Roosevelt Award by the National Collegiate Athletic Association, the organization's highest honor

1974 Among the first inductees into the National Track and Field Hall of Fame in Charleston, West Virginia

1976 Receives Medal of Freedom from President Gerald Ford (the highest honor that can be awarded to a civilian). President Ford tells Jesse, "Your character, your achievement, always will be a source of inspiration."

Devon Hind and Kate Bergstresser

1979 Receives the Living Legend Award from President Jimmy Carter

1980 March 31, dies from lung cancer in Tucson, Arizona

1982 The street leading to Olympic Stadium in Berlin is renamed, "Jesse Owens Allee"

1983 Elected to United States Olympic Hall of Fame

1988 President George Bush presents Ruth Owens with the Congressional Medal of Honor for Jesse's accomplishments in track, for his sincere patriotism and for his humanitarianism. President Bush says Jesse's accomplishments are "an unrivaled athletic triumph, but more than that, it really was a triumph for all humanity."

Jesse Owens: World's Fastest Human

About the Authors

Devon Hind began teaching and coaching after successful high school and college running careers. He taught physical education and coached varsity track and cross country teams at Berry High School in Hoover, Alabama from 1978-1981. He now teaches 8th grade science and coaches track and cross country at Simmons Middle School in Hoover. He holds a Bachelors Degree from the University of Alabama and an M.Ed. in Biology from the University of Alabama at Birmingham.

Kate Bergstresser is an aspiring author. She co-authored a book, *Unraked Hickory Nuts*, during her 8th grade year at Simmons Middle School in Hoover (with 9 other classmates). Kate is a student at Hoover High School. She runs cross country and track.

Devon Hind and Kate Bergstresser

Other Alabama Roots Biographies Available From Seacoast Publishing

Henry Aaron: Dream Chaser by Roz Morris
Hugo Black: Justice For All by Roz Morris
Paul Bryant:Football Legend by Sylvia B. Williams
Sam Dale: Alabama Pioneer by Tom Bailey
Daniel Pratt: Alabama's Great Builder by Tom Bailey
Emma Sansom: Confederate Hero by Margie Ross
Julia Tutwiler: Alabama Crusader by Roz Morris

Coming in the fall, 2002
Rosa Parks: Mother of the Civil Rights Movement
A.G. Gaston: Visionary Businessman
W.C. Handy: Father of the Blues

To order more copies of this or other Alabama Roots biographies, send 8.95 (includes postage) per book to:
Seacoast Publishing
P.O. Box 26492
Birmingham, AL 35260

Please print on your order the name and address where you wish the books to be shipped. Allow 15 days for delivery.
Orders also may be placed by telephone by calling 205.979.2909.

Jesse Owens: World's Fastest Human